MUSIC FROM THE MOTION PICTURE SOUNDTRACK   PIANO · VOCAL · GUITAR

PITCH PERFECT 2

T0070469

ISBN 978-1-4950-2997-4

HAL•LEONARD®
CORPORATION
7777 W. BLUEMOUND RD. P.O. BOX 13819 MILWAUKEE, WI 53213

Visit Hal Leonard Online at
www.halleonard.com

KENNEDY CENTER PERFORMANCE

Moderately

WE GOT THE WORLD
Words and Music by CAROLINE HJELT,
AINO JAWO, ELOF LOELV,
NICHOLE MORIER, LINUS EKLOW,
TOVE LO and SVIDDEN

TIMBER
Words and Music by ARMANDO CHRISTIAN PEREZ,
PEBE SEBERT, KESHA SEBERT, LUKASZ GOTTWALD,
HENRY WALTER, BREYAN STANLEY ISAAC,
PRISCILLA RENEA, JAMIE SANDERSON, LEE OSKAR,
KERI OSKAR and GREG ERRICO

AMERICA THE BEAUTIFUL
Words by KATHARINE LEE BATES
Music by SAMUEL A. WARD

WRECKING BALL

Words and Music by STEPHAN RICHARD MOCCIO,
MAUREEN McDONALD, SACHA SKARBEK,
LUKASZ GOTTWALD and HENRY WALTER

Yeah, I just closed my eyes and swung.

Left me crouch - ing in a blaze and fall.

All you ev - er did was wre - e - eck me.

me. (They say you're a freak.) You wre - e - eck me.

(stopping abruptly)

LOLLIPOP

Words and Music by
MIKA

*Recorded a half step higher.

Say love, say love, oh, love's gon-na get you down.)

Mom-ma told me what I should know: Too much can-

-dy gon-na rot your soul. If she loves you, let her go,

'cause love on-ly gets you down.

CAR SHOW

Serious Chorale

UPRISING

Words and Music by
MATTHEW BELLAMY

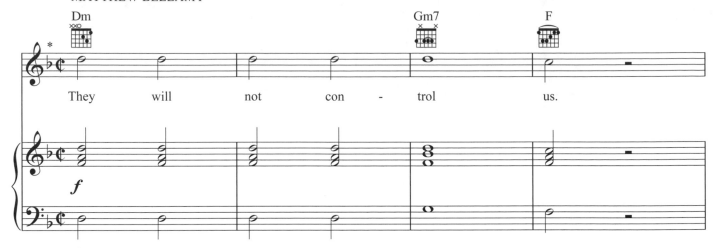

They will not con - trol us.

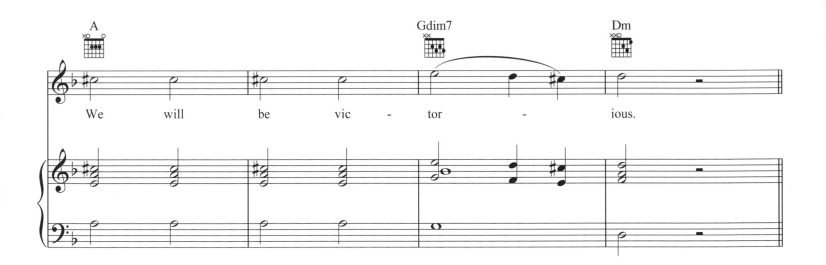

We will be vic - tor - ious.

A Cappella Groove

(Vocal percussion)

Recorded a half step higher.

TSUNAMI
Words and Music by ALEXANDER VAN DEN HOEF,
CHRISTOPHER VAN DEN HOEF, JOHN JAMES BORGER Jr.
and NILES HOLLOWELL-DHAR

Doo doo doo doo doo doo doo doo.

UPRISING
Words and Music by
MATTHEW BELLAMY

They will not force us.

They will stop de-grading us. (Come on.)

WINTER WONDERLAND/ HERE COMES SANTA CLAUS

WINTER WONDERLAND
Words by DICK SMITH
Music by FELIX BERNARD

HERE COMES SANTA CLAUS (RIGHT DOWN SANTA CLAUS LANE)
Words and Music by GENE AUTRY and OAKLEY HALDEMAN

lane, snow is glis-t'ning. A beau-ti-ful sight. We're

hap-py to-night, walk-ing in a win-ter won-der-land.

Here comes San-ta Claus, here comes San-ta Claus, right down San-ta Claus

lane; Vix-en and Blitz-en and all his rein-deer

Es - ki - mo way, __ walk-ing in a win - ter won - der - land.

Rap: *(See additional lyrics)*

Additional Lyrics

Rap: Once upon a time in the L.B.C.,
Santa came up missing; he was sitting by a tree.
His reindeers was near, but their leader wouldn't lead
So I took the lead. Now, as we proceed,...

This ain't for no mistletoe, but you need to listen, yo.
Just in case you didn't know, I call this my Christmas flow.
I could take you higher and higher. Chestnuts roast on an open fire.
"Gone away." Think that's what the, what the song says.

RIFF OFF

Moderately

THONG SONG
Words and Music by MARK ANDREWS,
DESMOND CHILD, MARQUIS COLLINS,
TIM KELLEY, BOB ROBINSON,
JOSEPH PAUL LONGO and ROBI ROSA

SHAKE YOUR BOOTY
Words and Music by HARRY CASEY
and RICHARD RAYMOND FINCH

LOW

Words and Music by TRAMAR DILLARD,
MONTAY HUMPHREY, KOREY ROBERSON,
HOWARD SIMMONS and T-PAIN

BOOTYLICIOUS

Words and Music by ROB FUSARI,
FALONTE D. MOORE, BEYONCE KNOWLES
and STEVIE NICKS

BABY GOT BACK
Words and Music by
ANTHONY L. RAY

LIVE LIKE YOU WERE DYING
Words and Music by TIM NICHOLS
and CRAIG WISEMAN

I went sky - div - ing, I went Rock - y Moun - tain climb - ing, I went two point sev - en sec - onds on a bull named Fu Man - chu. And I loved deep - er, and I spoke sweet - er, and I...

BEFORE HE CHEATS
Words and Music by JOSH KEAR
and CHRIS TOMPKINS

I dug my key in - to the side of his

A THOUSAND MILES
Words and Music by
VANESSA CARLTON

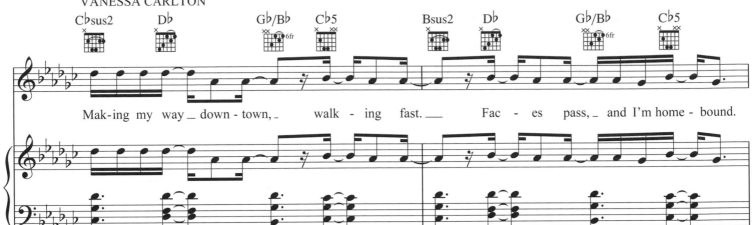

Mak-ing my way _ down-town, _ walk-ing fast. _ Fac-es pass, _ and I'm home-bound.

WE ARE NEVER GETTING BACK TOGETHER
Words and Music by TAYLOR SWIFT,
SHELLBACK and MAX MARTIN

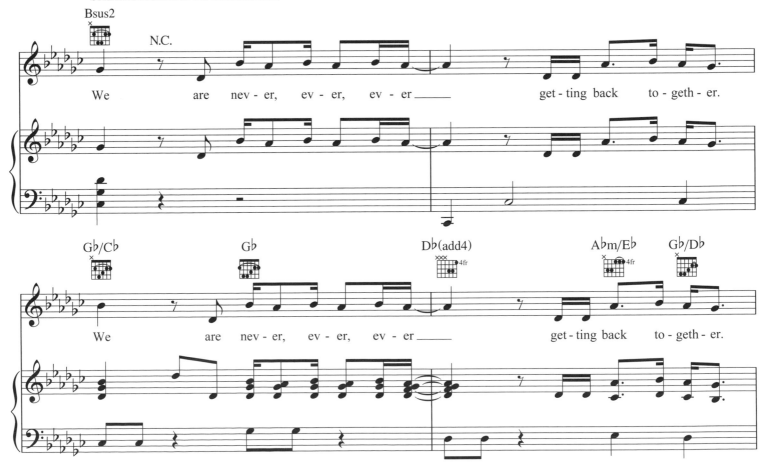

We are nev-er, ev-er, ev-er _____ get-ting back to-geth-er.

We are nev-er, ev-er, ev-er _____ get-ting back to-geth-er.

You go talk to your ___ friends, talk to my ___ friends, talk to me. ___ Well,

we are nev-er, ev-er, ev-er, ___ ev-er get-ting back to-

WHAT'S LOVE GOT TO DO WITH IT
Words and Music by GRAHAM LYLE
and TERRY BRITTEN

what's love ___ got to do, ___ got to do ___ with it?

geth-er.

What's love, ___ but a sec-ond-hand e-mo-tion? ___

THIS IS HOW WE DO IT
Words and Music by RICKY WALTERS,
OJI PIERCE and MONTELL JORDAN

Lyrics:

What's love ___ got to do, ___ got to do ___ with it?

Who needs a heart, when a heart can be bro-ken?

This is how we do it: ___ I'm

kind of buzzed, ___ and it's all be-cause ___ (this is how we do it). South

DOO WOP (THAT THING)
Words and Music by
LAURYN HILL

POISON
Words and Music by ELLIOT T. STRAITE

thing. _____ poi - son. _____ nev - er trust a big butt and a smile. That girl is poi - son. Here we

SCENARIO
Words and Music by JOHN DAVIS, ALI JONES-MUHAMMAD,
MALIK TAYLOR, BRYAN HIGGINS, JAMES JACKSON and TREVOR SMITH

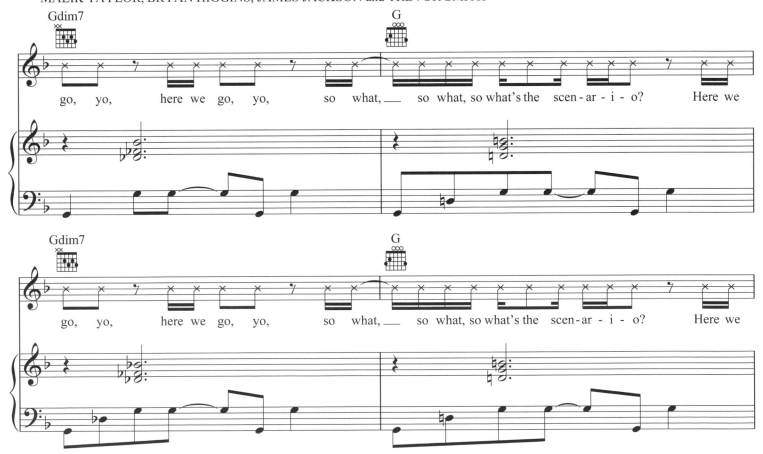

go, yo, here we go, yo, so what, ___ so what, so what's the scen - ar - i - o? Here we
go, yo, here we go, yo, so what, ___ so what, so what's the scen - ar - i - o? Here we

INSANE IN THE BRAIN
Words and Music by LOUIS FREEZE, SENEN REYES,
LARRY MUGGERUD and JERRY CORBITT

go. In - sane in the mem - brane. (In - sane in the brain.)

In - sane in the mem - brane. (In - sane in the brain.)

FLASHLIGHT
Words and Music by SIA FURLER, CHRISTIAN GUZMAN,
SAM SMITH, JASON MOORE and MARIO MEJIA

I've got all I need when I've got you and I, 'cause I look a - round me and see a sweet light.

I'm stuck in the dark, but you're my flash - light, get - ting me, get - ting me through the night.

JUMP

Words and Music by ALPHONSO MIZELL,
BERRY GORDY Jr., DEKE RICHARDS,
FREDDIE PERREN, JERMAINE DUPRI,
CLARENCE SATCHELL, GREGORY WEBSTER,
LEROY BONNER, MARSHALL JONES,
MARVIN PIERCE, NORMAN NAPIER,
RALPH MIDDLEBROOKS and WALTER MORRISON

Moderate Rap

Kris Kross will not be having anything today.   So as we stand here totally crossed out, we commence to make ya:

Jump, jump. The mack dad a make you.   Jump, jump. The dad-dy mack a make you.

Jump, jump, Kris Kross _ a make you.

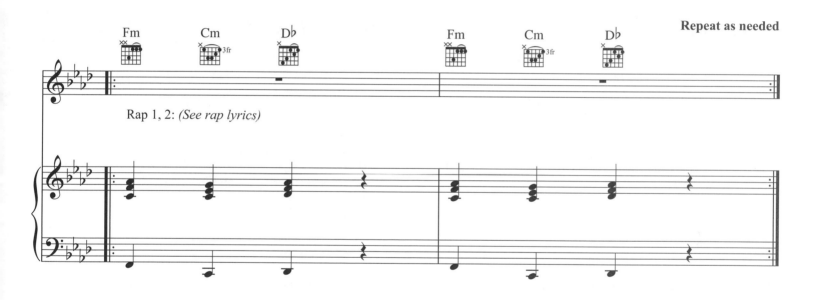

Repeat as needed

Rap 1, 2: *(See rap lyrics)*

Chorus

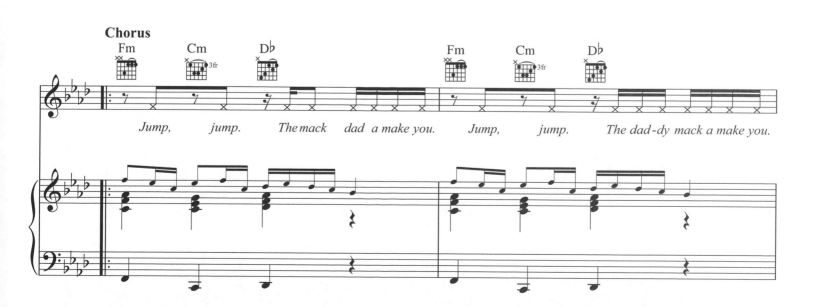

Jump, jump. The mack dad a make you. Jump, jump. The dad-dy mack a make you.

Rap Lyrics

Rap 1: Don't try to compare us 2 another bad little fad
I'm the mack and I'm bad
Given you something you never had
I make you bump, bump, wiggle and
Shake your rump
'Cause I be kickin' da flavor that makes
You wanna "Jump"

How high, real high
'Cause I'm just so fly
A young lovable, huggable
Type a guy
Everything is to the back
With a little slack
'Cause inside out is wigada,
Wigada, wigada, "Wack"

I come stumpin' with something pumpin'
To keep you jumpin'
R & B rappin' bull crap
Is what I'm dumpin'
Ain't nothing soft about Kris Kross
We all dat
So when they ask do they rock
Say believe dat
Chorus

Rap 2: I like my stuff knockin' "Knockin"
I love it when da girlies
Be like jockin', "Jockin'"
The D.A. double D.Y. M.A.C.
Yeah you know me
I got you jumpin' and bumpin' and pumpin'
Movin' all around "Gee"
I make the six step back
They dry to step to the mack
Then they got jacked
To the back you be sportin' your gear
Is that coincidental
"Act like you know and don't be claiming that it's mental"

Two li'l kids with a flow
You ain't never heard
Ain't nuttin' faking
You can understand every word
As you listen
To the smooth, smooth melody
The daddy makes you J.U.M.P.
Chorus

CONVENTION PERFORMANCE

Moderate groove

PROMISES

Words and Music by SONNY MOORE,
ALANA WATSON, DANIEL STEPHENS
and JOSEPH RAY

You've got me so___ wild, how can I ev-er de-ny?

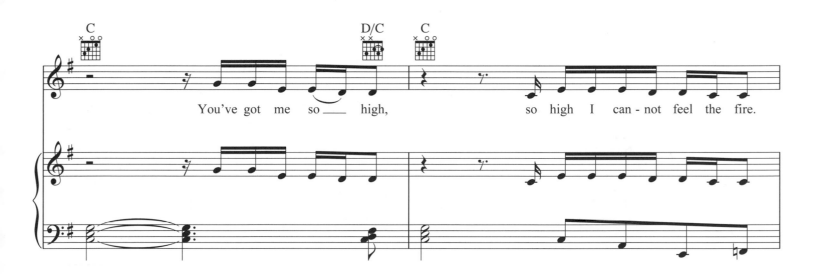

You've got me so___ high, so high I can-not feel the fire.

And you keep tell-ing me, tell-ing me that you'll be sweet

and you'll nev-er want to leave my side. As long as we don't break these prom-is-es ___ and they still feel all so wast-ed on ___ my-self. ___

Na na na na. I'm your

PROBLEM
Words and Music by NATALIA CAPPUCCINI,
JEFF BHASKER, GUILLAUME DOUBET and SKY MONTIQUE

dream girl, ___ this is real love. ___ But you know what they say a-bout me. That girl is a

prob - lem, girl is a prob - lem, girl is a prob - lem, prob - lem.
And they still feel all so wast - ed on my - self.

Sweat drip - ping down your chest, think - ing 'bout your tat - tooed knuck - les on my thigh, boy, boy, boy.

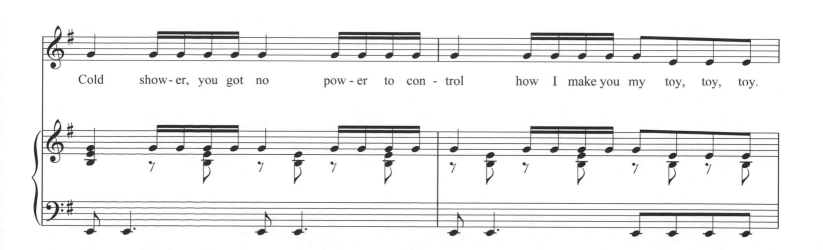

Cold show - er, you got no pow - er to con - trol how I make you my toy, toy, toy.

My hips rock-ing as we keep lip lock-ing, got the neigh- bors scream-ing e - ven loud - er, loud - er.

Lick me down like you were roll - ing riz - la, like I'm smok - ing, come and put me out. I'm your
So wast - ed on __ my- self. __

dream girl, _ this is real love. _ But you know what they say a - bout me. That girl is a

prob - lem, girl is a prob - lem, girl is a prob - lem, prob - lem. Oh, ba - by, you so

bad boy, _ drive me mad, boy. _ but you don't care what they say a - bout me. That girl is a

And they still feel all so wast - ed on __ my-self. ____

prob - lem, girl is a prob - lem, girl is a prob - lem, prob - lem.

BACK TO BASICS

Fast swing

BOOGIE WOOGIE BUGLE BOY
Words and Music by DON RAYE and HUGHIE PRINCE

YOU CAN'T HURRY LOVE
Words and Music by EDWARD HOLLAND Jr.,
LAMONT DOZIER and BRIAN HOLLAND

Moderate groove

it's a game of give and take ___ so break.

LADY MARMALADE
Words and Music by KENNY NOLAN
and ROBERT CREW

Hey sis- ter, go sis- ter, soul sis- ter, go sis- ter. It- chi git- chi ya ya da ___

___ da. ___ It- chi git- chi ya ya here. ___

Mo- cha cho- ca- la- ta ya ___ ya. ___ Cre- ole La- dy Mar - ma- lade. ___

MMMBOP

Words and Music by ISAAC HANSON,
TAYLOR HANSON and ZAC HANSON

MY LOVIN' (YOU'RE NEVER GONNA GET IT)
Words and Music by THOMAS McELROY and DENZIL FOSTER

WE BELONG

Words and Music by DANIEL ANTHONY NAVARRO
and DAVID ERIC LOWEN

ANY WAY YOU WANT IT
(WORLD CHAMPIONSHIP MEDLEY)

Words and Music by STEVE PERRY
and NEAL SCHON

Bollywood Indian Pop

WORLD CHAMPIONSHIP FINALE 1

Moderate R&B

MY SONGS KNOW WHAT YOU DID IN THE DARK (LIGHT EM UP)
Words and Music by ANDREW HURLEY, JOSEPH TROHMAN,
PATRICK STUMP, PETER WENTZ, BUTCH WALKER and JOHN HILL

Oh, _____ oh, _____ oh. _____

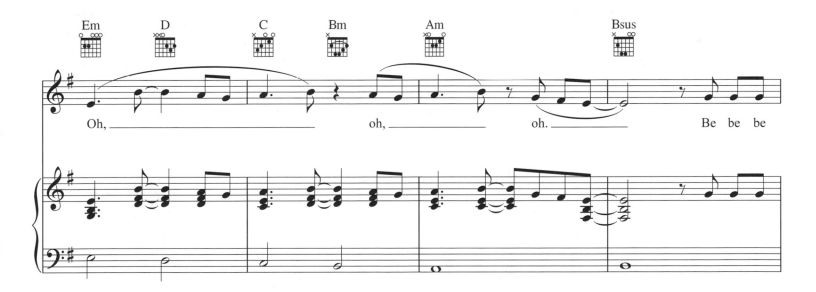

Oh, _____ oh, _____ oh. _____ Be be be

care-ful mak-ing wish-es in the dark, dark. Can't be sure when they'll hit their

Recorded a half step lower.

ALL I DO IS WIN

Words and Music by KHALED M. KHALED, T-PAIN, CALVIN BROADUS,
CHRISTOPHER BRIDGES, WILLIAM ROBERTS, JOHNNY MOLLINGS
and LEONARDO MOLLINGS

WORLD CHAMPIONSHIP FINALE 2

Moderately

RUN THE WORLD (GIRLS)
Words and Music by BEYONCE KNOWLES,
DAVE TAYLOR, THOMAS PENTZ,
NICK VAN DE WALL, ADIDJA PALMER
and TERIUS NASH

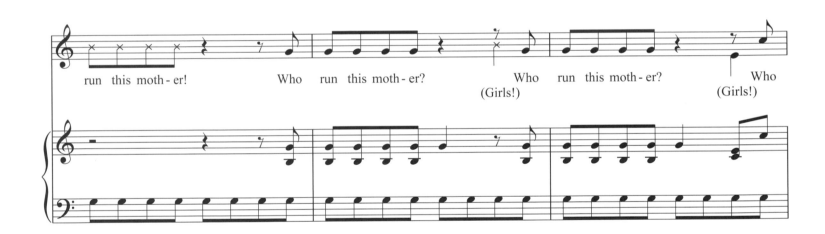

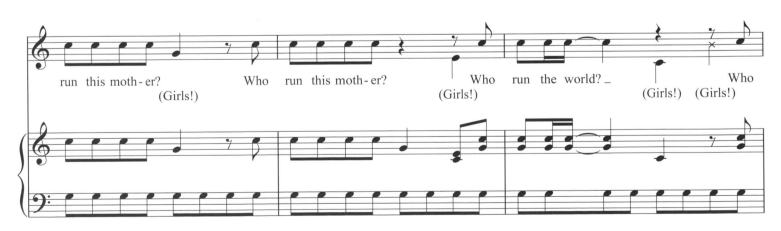

WHERE THEM GIRLS AT
Words and Music by TRAMAR DILLARD, OSCAR SALINAS,
JUAN SALINAS, GIORGIO TUINFORT, JARED COTTER,
ONIKA MARAJ, DAVID GUETTA, SANDY WILHELM
and MICHAEL CAREN

LADY MARMALADE
Words and Music by KENNY NOLAN and ROBERT CREW

run the world? _____ Where them girls at, girls at, girls at, girls at? We __ be -
(girls at, girls.)

WE BELONG
Words and Music by DANIEL ANTHONY NAVARRO
and DAVID ERIC LOWEN

long to the light; we be-long to the thun-der. We be - long,

TIMBER
Words and Music by ARMANDO CHRISTIAN PEREZ,
PEBE SEBERT, KESHA SEBERT, LUKASZ GOTTWALD,
HENRY WALTER, BREYAN STANLEY ISAAC, PRISCILLA RENEA,
JAMIE SANDERSON, LEE OSKAR, KERI OSKAR and GREG ERRICO

we be - long, we be - long to -
(It's go - in' down. I'm get - tin'

Slow groove

FLASHLIGHT

Words and Music by SIA FURLER,
CHRISTIAN GUZMAN, SAM SMITH,
JASON MOORE and MARIO MEJIA

FLASHLIGHT

Words and Music by SIA FURLER,
CHRISTIAN GUZMAN, SAM SMITH,
JASON MOORE and MARIO MEJIA

(cued note on repeat)

88